The Thorn of Your Name

Guichi lalu'

'These are stunning, halting, lilting poems of flesh and flower, of boulder and bone. Vivid and meditative, I hummed among their hills, they hummed in mine.'
– Inua Ellams, author of *The Actual*

'In Víctor Terán's poetry, the elements of nature are sentient, almost mischievous, and share blood ties with the people of Juchitán, the poet's birthplace and the father of the hurricane wind, the mother of the sun. The north wind raises its whip, trees laugh, the day gets fed up, the afternoon eats its meal, the clamour of winged ants announce the rains, the world opens up her thighs, while a white flower spurns no one. And within this universe, poems of love and resistance share in the ritual and celebrations, suffused with light and devotion: 'the lit tulip of your lips'; 'breath of god, / breath that lights and snuffs out / the candle flame / that is life.' In Shook's luminous translations, the emotions of longing open up their eyes in the night, alive and breathing as the moon: 'Delirious moon, like a colander / that dreams of overflowing with water.'
– Juana Adcock, author of *Split*

'These beautiful, subtle, sumptuous translations set alongside the original work make for a feast for the ears and the eyes alike.'
– Adam O'Riordan, author of *The Falling Thread*

Víctor Terán

The Thorn of Your Name

Guichi lalu'

Translated by Shook
from Spanish translations of the Isthmus Zapotec
made by the author

poetry
translation
centre

First published in 2024
by the Poetry Translation Centre Ltd
The Albany, Douglas Way, London, SE8 4AG

www.poetrytranslation.org

Poems © Víctor Terán 2024
English Translations © Shook 2024
Introduction © Shook 2024
Afterword © Leo Boix 2024

ISBN: 978-1-7384701-1-2
e-ISBN: 978-1-7384701-2-9

A catalogue record for this book is available from the British Library

Typeset in Minion by Poetry Translation Centre Ltd

Series Editor: Erica Hesketh
Cover Design: Kit Humphrey
Printed in the UK by T.J. Books Limited

The PTC is supported using public funding by
Arts Council England

Supported using public funding by
**ARTS COUNCIL
ENGLAND**

Contents

Introduction

Born in Juchitan, Oaxaca in 1958, Víctor Terán writes in an Indigenous language whose written tradition includes both one of the most ancient undeciphered scripts in Mesoamerica and a robust contemporary canon of poetry, novels, and other contemporary forms. Author of six volumes of poetry, including an anthology of his own translations of 40 world poets into Isthmus Zapotec, as well as two volumes of short stories, Terán stands as one of present-day Mexico's preeminent Indigenous voices. In his writing and his work as a language activist he has long advocated for the recognition of the intrinsic value of the Zapotec language and for its expanded use in every domain of contemporary Indigenous life.

I first encountered Terán's poetry in 2008, after visiting Zapotec communities in the Central Valley and Pacific highlands regions of Oaxaca. Thrilled at discovering a contemporary poet with such an immediately recognizable voice, I translated his poem 'The North Wind Whips' as soon as I finished reading its last line, working initially from Terán's own translation into Spanish, which I soon learned he had been forced to make himself for lack of literary translators from Zapotec.

Terán's poems seemed to me inseparable from the landscape of his hometown of Juchitan, an Indigenous town of around 100,000 people on the southern edge of Oaxaca's narrow Isthmus of Tehuantepec, skirted by farming communities as well as the fishermen who rely on the nearby sea for their livelihoods. As I have lived with, performed and revised these poems over the course of 15 years – and having shared meals and mezcals at Terán's table in Juchitan – I have come to believe that the ubiquity of place in Terán's poetry is only one manifestation of a bidirectional relationship, and that Terán's language – the Isthmus Zapotec language itself, known to its speakers as diidxazá – is itself an essential part of the landscape of Juchitán, 'curlew that sings and dances in Zapotec'.

With the encouragement of the British poet Jamie McKendrick, who introduced me to Sarah Maguire and the Poetry Translation Centre, I continued to read and translate Terán – and to barrage him with my questions. Continuing in the same mode as we began, I would render initial versions from Terán's own Spanish, then revise after receiving his responses to my lists of queries, which sought to better understand how the poem worked in Zapotec. To some degree, I was aided in this endeavor by my background in generative linguistics and linguistic anthropology, as well as the time I had spent in Indigenous communities in rural Oaxaca and Guerrero. Still, my curiosity, frankness, and willingness to test the limits of the adage that there's no such thing as a stupid question likely proved the greater assets, along with my desire to ensure that I was doing right by the Isthmus Zapotec language itself.

Today there are about half a million speakers of Zapotec, spread across 58 variants with varying degrees of mutual intelligibility – often less than exists between the Romance languages, for example. Most are considered endangered or in decline, including Terán's Isthmus variant, whose speakers today number 100,000. Terán considers the production of culture in Isthmus Zapotec to be a cornerstone of its preservation, serving as a manifestation and record of Zapotec experience, encouraging the development of neologisms and expanding the language's use cases to correspond to the contemporary Indigenous experience, and inspiring the youth, whose use and transmission of the language is the fragile rampart against its displacement by Spanish. To my surprise, my translations have played a small role in that fortification. When I visited Terán's home in 2011, I was happy to see a copy of *Poems/Diidxado'*, our 2010 Poetry Translation Centre chapbook, in his living room. Upon picking it up, I noticed that the paper stock was distinct from the copies we had received from the PTC. I asked about the discrepancy, and Terán told me that there had been so much demand for the book in Juchitan that he himself had printed a bootlegged edition to distribute to readers and friends. 'Can anyone read the English translations?' I asked, still not entirely understanding.

'No,' he said, 'but it makes them so proud to see that the wider world considers Zapotec poetry deserving of translation'.

In 2022, Terán revised the entirety of his self-translations into Spanish. He tells me that he believes he has become a better poet in Spanish over the course of his life, thanks largely to his reading of Spanish-language poetry, and that he now translates more freely than when he first began, when he often prioritized syntactic reflection of the Zapotec over the idiomatic. It is true that his revised versions sparkle with renewed life, often eschewing more flowery language in favor of the immediacy of the image or the orality of intimate expression. While reading these new versions sometimes inspired new lines of questioning about the underlying Zapotec, I seldom felt I needed to update the English to reflect the Spanish; in many cases, my versions already employed simpler or more conversational language, as a result of our discursive back-and-forth. To me this offered a small proof that our process had worked. Still, there are instances where I feel I have improved my earlier versions over time, often by economizing phrases or reworking syntax to render more natural constructions in English, as in the language of break-ups the poet imitates near the end of 'Your Memory'.

I have now lived with Terán's poems for fifteen years, and I have heard him read his poetry aloud many dozens of times, to the point that I have inadvertently memorized several, the lilting cadence of his Zapotec seared into my memory. This experience, as well as reading aloud my English translations to audiences all over the USA and UK, has proved immensely helpful, sharpening my meter and enabling me to better match my pacing to Terán's.

The Thorn of Your Name is the most thematically represent-ative selection of Terán's poems yet in English, and includes a handful of poems translated into English for the first time. Terán himself conceives of his poetry as belonging to three broad categories: 'poems of longing for [his] hometown and people', love poems, and poems of protest. My goal with this selection was to showcase all three, a subtle redress to my own work to date as Terán's translator and advocate in English. I had previously focused on Terán's iconic love poems, which are still well represented here, as that is his predominant mode, and one that generally requires little context or explanation because of its grounding in the imagistic, as in the chilling final lines of 'Your Name':

> I'll no doubt have one last breath
> capable of filling a basket of winged ants
> that will proclaim my love
> like the commotion that announces
> coming rains.

Terán's pride in and love for Zapotec culture, land, and language are displayed in poems like 'I Am Native to These Lands', and throughout his poetry in his mention of Zapotec customs and regional flora like the chintul seed, used to clean and condition women's hair. 'Soldiers', meanwhile, dedicated to the disappeared teacher and worker advocate Víctor Pineda Henestrosa (whose daughter Irma Pineda has become a major poet of the generation just below Terán's, and is translated into English by Wendy Call), exemplifies his protest poetry. The poems in this selection display how these three modes overlap throughout Terán's work – and one must remember that the very act of writing in an Indigenous language is itself a radical political act in defiance of centuries of displacement, oppression and genocide.

This selection also includes a sampling of Terán's haiku, which he has written, along with tanka, for over 30 years, since first discovering Basho, whom he has also translated into Zapotec. Unlike the majority of our English-language tradition of the form, he has eschewed the syllable-based rules of Japanese prosody in his development of the Isthmus Zapotec haiku, and I have followed his lead in English. Terán has expressed to me that he believes the Zapotec language to be particularly well suited to the pithiness of the form, and, beyond that, that Zapotec thinking is similarly grounded in the natural world and therefore likewise attuned to the changing of the seasons. Standing in direct contrast to the parochialism historically assumed of Indigenous poets by the allegedly cosmopolitan poets of Mexico City's literary establishment, these haiku are just one example of Terán's engagement with a wide range of world literature. (Indeed his own translations, typically made from Spanish intermediaries, range from Hikmet to Wordsworth, and even include Carol Ann Duffy!)

In an essay about his calling to write poetry in an Indigenous language, published in the Poetry Translation Centre's recent anthology *Living in Language*, Terán writes, 'My singing, then, is not only for readers in my language, but for the world…' I feel so fortunate to have played a role in sharing them with you by making them sing in English.

Shook, Newt Beach, 2024

Poems

Lalu'

Ridxí' ne huaxhinni, lá lu'.
Siadó', huadxí, lu gueela'
nisi lá lu' riree xieque
ndaani' bichuga íque'
sica tuuxa zeguyoo
runi biniti guendabiaani',
nisi lá lu' riree chuuchi
lu ludxe'
sica benda ndaani' ná'
ti guuze'.

Guindisa' ti gui'chi', lá lu',
cuaque' ti xiixa, lá lu'.
Gabati' nalu' nuaa'
cadi daabi guichi lá lu'
íque bicuini naya',
ne ratiicasi zedide'
málasi gó la'na'
guendarietenala'dxi' lú lu'
ñee xquendanabane'.

Ma yanna nga nabaana
ne huidxe mápeca saa guidxi.
Zándaca ridxí zaxhaca la'dxi'
sá' nanda huaxhinni.
Zándaca naa guibane' ti dxi
ne guirá' ca yaya xtí' xquendagute',

12

Your Name

Day and night, your name.
In the morning, the afternoon, at dusk
only your name spins
through my head
like a man straight-jacketed
for having lost his mind,
only your name slips
over my tongue
like a fish between the hands
of a fisherman.

I lift a paper, your name.
I put something away, your name.
There is nowhere I go
that I do not have the thorn of your name
nailed to the tip of my finger,
and no matter where I go
the memory of your face silently bites
the leg of my existence.

It is time for Lent
and May's fiestas are near.
Perhaps the day is fed up
with chasing the night.
Maybe one day I'll wake up
to the scandal of my death.

zapa ruaʼ ti nisadóʼ guendaricaalaʼdxiʼ
ndaaniʼ ladxiduaʼ guzeeteʼ lá luʼ,
zápaʼ ruaʼ neca xtuudxi huiiniʼ bi
guzayaniáʼ ti dxumisú birixhiaa
gusitenalaʼdxiʼ lii guendaranaxhii stinneʼ
sica rusietenalaʼdxiʼ laanu ne xquendayaya
dxi ma zeedadxiña xhí nisaguié.

Despite it all I'll have an ocean of sighs
in my soul, to whisper your name.
I'll no doubt have one last breath
capable of filling a basket with winged ants
that will proclaim my love
like the commotion that announces
coming rains.

Xavizende, badudxaapa' huiini' rudxeela'

Xavizende,
badudxaapa' huiini' rudxeela',
guie' quichi' qui gapa xiladxi'
sica xpiaani' gubidxa,
guie' quichi' rindá' naxhi do'
sica ti le' xunaxi.
Nadxiee' lii
ti qui runibia'lu' guendanaguibi',
ti qui gannu' pa nuu guendarachelú sti' stobi.
Naro'ba' ladxido'lo', rudii nalu' tutiica;
pa chu' huaxa tu laa guchachaladi,
bisiá tica lii, ti guidxi beedxe'.

Xavizende,
yu'du' ró' xti' ca binnizá,
guidxi guie' qui runibiá' guendaridxaga,
guidxi guie nanna nuu guendarituí lú.
Paraa qui guindisa' lalu' ya',
paraa qui guzaabe' larindxó' lalu' lu bi;
dani gui guirá'si dxi caniibidxacha,
nisa gue'la' nexhedxí cayuunda' mudubina ndaani'.

Xavizende,
bixhoze bi yooxho', jñaa gubidxa.
Chegorio Melendre ne Binu Gada
bilaadxica' guie' íquelu'.
Che Gome ne Víctor Yodo

Juchitan, My Bride

Juchitan,
my bride,
white flower who spurns no one
like the light of the sun,
white flower with your heavenly scent
like a garden of brides.
I love you
because you know no avarice,
because you're oblivious to envy.
Your kindness is vast, you extend your hand to all;
but if someone takes advantage of your openness
you transform into an eagle, into a harsh people.

Juchitan,
greatest temple of the Zapotecs,
cordial people who know no fatigue,
tough people unaware of shame.
How can I not eulogize your name!
How can I not raise the sacred banner of your name on the winds!
Volcano in perpetual eruption,
immense water in clear calm, rich with water lilies.

Juchitan,
father of the hurricane wind, mother of the sun.
José Gregorio Meléndez and Albino Jiménez
crown your greatness.
José Gómez and Víctor Pineda

cuzaanica' neza zizalu'.
La'guiaa tica ná' ca binniñaa
ne binni guuze' stilu',
xhiaa biulú ñee ca gunaa xiiñu'.
Xavizende ró, Xavizende huiini':
berelele ruunda' ne ruyaa diidxazá,
gunaa cha'hui' ruunané ca xiiñi',
binnigola zá, bixhoze biida'.

light your way.
The arms of your peasants and fishermen
are made of steel,
the feet of your women, hummingbird wings.
Big Juchitan, small Juchitan:
curlew that sings and dances in Zapotec,
loving mother confident to comfort her children,
ancient son of the clouds, my grandfather.

Lii

Ca bisilana' cha'hui' bizalulu',
guie' xiñá'rini guidiruaalu',
ca xuba' huiini' quichi' láyalu',
ca guitu bidola xhídxilu',
ca beelaxiaa dxitaxa'nalu',
guendaxunu ladeñeelu',
guie'xhuuba' naxhi xquéndalu',
ruuti yaa ca naa.

You

Your noble calupin cherry eyes,
the lit tulip of your lips,
the white kernels of corn that are your teeth,
the round calabashes of your chest,
the cottony flesh of your hips,
the mamey between your legs,
the fragrant jasmine of your being,
by dying kill me.

Biguié'

Bi yooxho',
bi nanda,
bi guie'biguá,
bi gu'xhubidó':
Biguié'.

Ra lídxi ca gue'tu' cubi
zusichaahui' lu bidó':
zusiguaa xiiñibiduaa,
zanda cuananaxhi;
zacá beedxebiyé', naze guie'daana'
ne guie'biguá;
za'ta' daa, daapa cuananaxhi,
guendaró ne nisacha'hui' lú.

Gu'xhubidó', libana
ne tapa gui'ri' ro',
zusindá' naxhi ne zuzaani'
neza gueeda ne ché'
ca biuuza' gue'tu';
ca ni guedané ne chiné
ca ndaaya' rusieche'
laanu ne diuxi.

Bi guie' lubí,
bi gue'tu',
bi ndaaya',

Feast of the Dead

Impetuous primeval wind,
cold season,
of the scent of marigolds,
of exquisite incense:
Feast of the Dead.

In the house of the just departed
they adorn the saints' table:
raise banana trees
and decorate them with fruits;
the frame presides, lined with green leaves
and yellow marigolds;
in the center of the arrangement the reed mat
brims with fruits and delicacies.

Clouds of copal, prayers,
and four candles
perfume and illuminate
the path trodden by
the visiting dead,
who bring and take away
the blessings that influence
our life and the gods.

Scent of flowers in the air,
season of the dead,
of consecration,

bi ruaa bidó,
bi rusibani ne rusuí
xpele gui'ri' guendanabani.

breath of god,
breath that lights and snuffs out
the candle flame that is life.

Biete bi

Biete bi.
Lu neza gui'chi' ne bacuela
nanda saaca' ne xiana.
Ruguubeedxe' ca yoo,
ridopa cuuxhu' bi'cu'.
Daabi ti xiixa
bicuininá' huadxí ri':
ti guichi guluxu,
ti guiiba' tini.

Nuu tu laa
gudu'ba' xhaata' gueza guibá',
bisaana ni naté, nagu'xhu'.
Xaguete' ri' guiruti'
nibeezá xpandá',
guirá' zeguyoo ra lidxi
cugaba' xquenda zí'.

Caxidxi zinña,
laaca tuuxa biaanatá'
gudxite xcunaa laa.

Yanadxí guirá'
bietenala'dxi' ladeñee,
málasi gunna binni
nuu guendaruseegu' ra lidxi.

The North Wind Whips

The north wind whips through.
In the streets trash and leaves
are chased with resentment.
Houses moan,
dogs curl into balls.
There is something
in the afternoon's finger:
a catfish spine,
a rusty nail.

Someone unthinkingly
smoked cigarettes in heaven,
left it overcast, listless.
Here at ground level no one can
take their shadow for a walk,
sheltered in their houses, people
are surprised to discover their misery.

The palms snicker
at a lover betrayed,
left waiting in vain.

Today the world
agreed to open her thighs,
and the townspeople understand
they must sometimes close their doors.

Tu laa nanna
xiñee cazaaca' huadxí di',
xiñee nisi nuaa'
gudxiga' guiiba' ladxidó'
bazeendu' ni bixhague'
ruaa ca bi di' yanadxí,
xiñee nisi nuaa'
gudxiga' yaana' xii
bixé' cundubi rarí.

Cuxidxi ca yaga,
riaba riásaca'
cuxidxica' naa
runi biaanata'ya'.

Latané naa nagasi
guirá' manihuiini' ruunda'
guidxélatu lu yaga,
ti gabe' laatu
pa naye'que' guichalaga binidxaba'.

Who can divine
why I meditate on this afternoon?
Why is it birthed in me
to knife the heart
of the spirit who uncovered the mouth
of the now whipping wind,
to jam corncobs in the nose
of the ghost that pants outside?

The trees roar with laughter,
they split their sides,
they celebrate
that you never arrived.

Now bring me
the birds
you find in the trees,
so I can tell them
if the devil's eyelashes are curled.

Ndaani’ batanaya’

Ndaani’ batanaya’
cayó huadxí ri’:
mani’ té bilaa runi ma’ bio’xho’,
mani’ guude, mani’ biidi’.

Nexhe’ ti neza lase’
deche dani rihuinni rarica’,
lubí chonna bayu’ quichi’
ziyuí̱ca’, ziyuí̱ca’,
riluí̱ cuzabinaca’ luá’.
Nugaanda guendaribana’
xquixhe ndaani’ ladxiduá’,
ne guendananala’dxi’
cutuxhu lugu’ xquiiba’.

Rietetí layú rarí’,
layú guichi, layú guie.
Guxhu’ ne za rihuinni,
za, gu’xhu’ ne guendananá.

Neza lase’ ziyeeque’
deche dani rica’,
neza lase’ riné ra lídxilu’.
Za yu’la’ biaa guibá’ ca la?
zándaca cayuuyu’ ní,
zándaca cayuuyu’ ní,
cadi bia’ za ca nga xquendaranaxhiee’,
cadi bia’ za ca.

From the Palm of My Hand

From the palm of my hand
the afternoon eats its meal:
lean horse abandoned in old age,
nagging horse, dirty horse.

There is a trail
behind the hill you see there.
In the open sky
three white tissues blow away,
waving goodbye.
Nostalgia has hung
its hammock in my heart,
and my grudges
diligently sharpen their weapons.

Here the earth is broken,
land of acacias and stones.
Smoke and clouds are visible,
clouds, smoke, and grief.

The footpath that zigzags
behind that hill
leads to your house.
The long cloud spanning the horizon –
perhaps you're looking at it,
perhaps you're looking at it now.
My love for you is not the size of that cloud,
not that size.

Guidúbilu' runebia'ya'

Guidúbilu' runebia'ya',
guidúbinaca peou'.
Pa ñácalu' ti guidxi
ratiicasi ninabadiidxa' cabe náa
naa nulué' pa neza riaana ní.
Riuuládxepea' guidúbilu',
riuuladxe' guuya' guiní'lu', guxídxilu',
guzeque yannilu'. Dxiña yaga guiropa' dani
zuguaa ndí' xtilu', ra guyaa' dxiqué
rigucaa' ruaa bidó'. Ñacaladxe' rua'
ñuá' ne niree ndaani' guixhidó' xtilu',
ni guya' dxiiña' guiluxe guendanabani ndaani'.
Biza'naadxi' bido' guzana lii, qui gápalu'
ra guidiiñeyulu'. Binnindxó' nga naa
ti bibane' lii, guca' lii. Yanna ma cadi naa
ridxiiche' gudxigueta lú ca nguiii ra zedi'dilu',
ma cadi naa racalugua' cueelu' lari.
Ti bidxiña lubí nga lii, ti balaaga' guie'
ziguite yeche' lu guiigu' ti siadó'.

Gabati' lii nou' qui ñunebia'ya', nou'
qui ñuuladxe'. Pa ñándasi ñácarua'
biaani' ruxheleruaa ruuya' ca nduni
yuxido' quichi' beelaxa'nalu'. Pa ñándasi
nibeza rua'
            ndaani' guidxi sicarú
                        ni nácalu'.

I Know Your Body

I know your body,
entirely I know you.
If you were a city
I could give perfect directions
to wherever they asked me.
I like all of your body,
I like to see you talk, laugh,
move your head. Your two well-rounded hills
are the honey of bees, where I would go to honor the gods.
I would have liked to continue coming to your forest,
lodgings deliberately built for an ideal death.
You were created with love,
your body is worthy of praise. What an honor to have lived,
to have existed. I am no longer bothered
when men turn to look at you,
I am no longer impatient when you undress.
You are a stag in the air, a raft of flowers
that snakes across the river by morning.

There is no part of your body I do not know, there is no
part I do not like. I want to keep being
the light stunned as it glances off your white,
luscious form. I want to keep
living
        in the beautiful city
                    that you are.

33

Huadxi que ziyaba

Biluuza ti ridxi
ndaani' yánilu',
ti ridxi naxiñá'
guizá' dxichi
bitubi lu luuna'.

Huadxí que ziyaba,
gunna ni naa
ti lu neza binadia'ga' zixidxi
chuppa guidibo'co' nayeche'.

Bindaate' xpié'
cue'diágalu'
laga ca naya' naazedxiichi',
ziyuí' xtípaca', ziguxooñe' naca',
ziyabaneca' naa guidxilayú.

Huadxí que ziyaazi',
gunna' dxindxe' piá'
ti biiya' cayábayati
ca lágalu'.

The Afternoon Fell

From your throat
a broken cry,
a red cry
entirely whole
writhed on the bed.

The afternoon fell,
I knew
because of the two brave shoes
that echoed through the street.

I spilled my breath
over your shoulders,
while my vigorous and headstrong hands
grew weak, lowering your body
until it was one with mine on the floor.

The afternoon was sinking,
I knew it fully
by the slow movement
of your eyelids.

Dxuca'

Icaa Víctor Yodo

Xiñee zinetu
dxuca',
badunguiiu guichi zundí'
stiidxa'
ribana la'dxi'
Guidxiguie' stinne'.

Dxuca',
xi bi'nibe laatu?
Bixhatañeebe
yanni binnilídxitu la?
Bitúxhube xpi'cube
luguiá' bacaandaguie'
stitu la?

Dxuca',
lagabi naa,
cadi góyaatu diidxa'
redandá
lu lúdxitu.

Dxuca',
la guxhele ruaa.

Soldiers

For Víctor Pineda Henestrosa[1]

Why,
soldiers,
did you kidnap
a man whose word is as true
as a thorn,
who yearns for
my Juchitán de las flores?

Soldiers,
what grievance did he commit against you?
Did he stomp
on your family's necks?
Did he set his dogs on
your flowered dreams?

Soldiers,
tell me,
don't bite the words
that rise
to your tongues.

Soldiers,
open your mouths.

---

1. A teacher and advocate for rural workers, kidnapped by the Mexican Army
on 11th July 1978

Bibaneniá' lalu'

Bibaneniá' lalu' naga' ndaani' yanne'.
Pa niní' ca naya' ni guniéxcaanda'
ñuuyapiá' nusabalú diuxi.
Bandaa cayuni xhiiña' lu gueela'
sica ti gubaana' biziidichaahui'.
Ne lu bi za'bi' guendaruyadxí bana' xtinne'
naaze nanda guidiruaa.

Gasti' nou' qui runebia'ya' ndaani' yoo ra nuaa'
ne zacá ladxiduá' cayacaditi
sica ti xcuidi guladxi bi'cu'.
Rahuayaa bicuininá' xquendabiaane'
ti guibani chaahui'.
Laga ti gayuaa bigose buubu
ziyásanene lu layú ladxiduá'.

Ze'gu' lu beeu huaxhinni.
Naaze guppa larigueela' yaase' xtí' guibá.
Pa ñanna' caniéxcaanda' qui nundaa' ca nalu',
pa ñanna' zabane' niguiidxedxiiche' lii ti que ñelu'.
Rigui'ba' ti yuuba' ra yanne'
ne ricaa runi xtí' ladxiduá'.

Paraa nda' nuu ca luyaande sicarú lu' ya',
paraa nda' ca guidiruaalu'.
Biaanaru' xiixa xtinne'

I Woke With Your Name

I woke with your name stuck in my throat.
If my hands told of what I dreamed last night
I am certain god would lower his gaze.
The termite labors at night
like an experienced thief.
And my languid face hangs in the air,
lips lightly trembling.

There is nothing in this house I do not know
but even so my heart quivers
like a child chased by a dog.
I bite my understanding's feet
to wake it from its stupor.
A flock of rooks
lifts into flight, slowly, from the empty field of my soul.

It's night and the moon is obscured.
The humidity suffocates the black sheet of the sky.
If I had known I was dreaming I would not have let go of
    your hands,
if I had known I would have held you so you wouldn't leave.
A pain rises up my throat
and clenches my heart.

Where do your big, beautiful eyes walk about,
where your lips walk?
Does anything of mine still

ndaani' ladxidó'lo' la?
Huandí' nga ma' biaanda' lii
ni gúcanu la?

Bibaneneá' lalu' naga' ndaani' yanne'.

exist inside your heart?
Can it be that you'll forget
all we were?

I woke with your name stuck in my throat.

Bixidu'

Ti dxumi benda.
Chupa guixhe niza.
Chonna bixidu'.

Bindaate', gudiibi.
Bichuxhi, guxuuba'.
Dané naa ne zaa guti.

Kisses

A basket of fish.
Two nets bursting with corncobs.
Three kisses.

Upturn it, clean them.
Husk them, strip their kernels.
Give them to me, then you can die.

Yude' cuyaa

Yudé cuyaa galaabato' ná' tapa neza.
Ca yaga nagá' caguíteca' tu jmá naguudxi deche.
Ladxiduá' nexhegaa lu luuna' cabeza lii, bezaluá' zuba,
rinaaze' bi guichaíque, zuba, cugaba' panda bihui
culaa xii ti xcuidi zubaxuuna'.

Laga lii ya', xi cayuni ndou' nagasi.
Nannu' xiinga guendaribeza ti gunaa
gueeda guxhídxiná'
lu gande iza xtí' ti badunguiiu la?

Yudé cuyaa galaabato' bizaluá'.
Ti mani' canareeguite ndaani' ca nezarini xtinne'.
Gunaa bazeendu', xi binidxaba' cayu'nu' qui gueedu'.
Ma' bigaba' birá bicuininá' gubidxa,
bi yooxho' ma' bigani lu neza, bidxaga ruaa,
cachuundu', ma' nacahui guibá',
ndaani' naya' nexheguundu' guguhuiini'
guleza lii.

Whirlwind

The whirlwind stirs up the street's dust.
The trees compete to make the most elegant curtsies.
My heart stretched across the bed, waiting for you, eyes still,
the air tousles my hair, still, the pigs announce
their attack on the boy squatting to do his business.

And you, what might you be doing at this instant?
Do you by chance know what it's like to wait for a woman
who promised a twenty-year-old man
she would knock on his door?

The dust dances on the empty lot of my eyes.
A chestnut romps through my blood's pathways.
Perverse woman, where the hell are you, what the hell are
    you doing?
I've tired of counting the sun's fingers,
the gust, fatigued, has stopped provoking the street.
It's twilight, the sky dark with shadow.
In my hands it lies dying,
the turtledove that dreamed of cooing you to sleep.

Beeu

Beuu. Beeu quichi' sicarú
sica biaani' bizalú ti zí'
gudiñelaga ti lempa ndaani' gui'xhi'.

Beeu bilumbu' riga ca bé.
Beeu ndaani' ti gunaa nacaxiiñi'.
Beeu qui gapa guendabiaani'
sica ti bidxadxa nisa.

Beeu dxita gudi'di' xhí.
Beeu gulabere' mboolo' güi lu yaga:
bisiga'de' naa tindaa xquendanayéchelu'
gusigaanda' xquedanabani xquidxe'.

Beeu bidaaniquichi'
biaa íque ti xunaxi binnizá:
bisiga'de' naa ca bacuzaguí ladxido'lo'
guzaani' neza sá' ca xpinne'.

Beeu guizá', beeu dxa'tipa.
Beeu cuxidxisá
ne cagapaxa'na'.

Moon

Moon. Sweet white moon
like the gleam in the eye of a luckless hunter
chasing a rabbit across the mountain.

Moldy cachimbo rind moon.
Pregnant belly moon.
Delirious moon, like a colander
that dreams of overflowing with water.

Deformed-egg moon.
Ripe rubber-fruit moon:
give me a slice of your joy
to bring my town back to life.

Ceremonial huipil moon
that adorns the Zapotec woman's head:
give me the fireflies that live in your heart
to light my people's paths.

Moon intact, full moon.
Moon cackling in joy,
slapping both knees.

Binnihuala'dxi'nga naa

Binnihuala'dxi' nga naa,
gule' ndaani' Guidxiguie',
rini xti' ca gula'sa' neá'
ne ludxe' ruunda' diidxaguie'.

Nanna' xi neza zaya'
ne nanna' pa raa nga zeaa',
neca guiaba guí zindaya',
rini xti' binnibisiá neá'.

Nadxiee' guirá' ca xquenda'
casi nadxiee' diidxazá,
ne rabe' xtiidxa' risaca
bia'ca risaca diidxaxtiá.

Guiranu binnihuala'dxica'
gusisácanu laanu,
ndaani' guidxilayú di'
bia'ca risaca guiranu.

Binni rusiaanda' tu laa
lu bi rizá renda xquipi,
binni rusiaanda' tu laa
ririga ne riniti.

I Am Native to These Lands

I am native to these lands,
I was born in Juchitán,
I carry Zapotec blood
and my tongue casts wide
the sweetness of its source.

I know where I come from
and I know where I'm headed,
though it rains I'll arrive aflame,
my blood the blood of eagle-men.

I love and respect my culture,
my diidxazá language,
and I proclaim my tongue as valuable
as the Spanish tongue.

We First Peoples
make our value known,
in all the universe
no culture is superior to any other.

Those that forget their origin –
their navels wander in the air,
those who forget their essence
wring out their souls and submit.

Gaayu' haicú

Bi yooxho' ne saa,
bizuudi' guie' ze' zeeda:
ma nuaa' Guidxiguie'.

*

Biaba nisaguié,
nabiidi' nuu nisadó',
zo'no' bendabuaa.

*

Cayuuna' bi' cu',
nuchiaa gueelado' suudi,
caguba' gueza.

*

Xho' naxhi i'cu',
sica rindá' guie' ne yu:
guche zapandú.

Five Haiku

Sweet breeze and fiestas,
jubilant underskirts:
I've arrived in Juchitan.

*

It rained,
the sea is scrambled,
we will eat shrimp.

*

Dogs howl,
the thick night spreads its petticoat,
I smoke a cigarette.

*

The celestial scent of your hair,
essence of flower and field:
the chintul has blossomed.

*

Bilaa ca bi'cu'
nándaca' pa bi pa za,
careza guibá.

*

The dogs have been loosed,
chasing the wind or the clouds,
thunder in the heavens.

Xhiuuba' be

Nutaabi yuuba' guendarietenala'dxi' ladxiduá'
cue' lindaa huadxí te di'.
Nuu tu zuba caguiba xquendanayeche'
xa'na' yaga baca'nda xti' ti guendaranaxhii la?
Guidxilayú di' naca ti dxia naro'ba' qui gapa xhibia'
candaabi' lu xté diuxi.
Binidxaba' canaguyaa lu neza
laga ti bi'cu' nagola
zixupila'na' xcuaana' gundagaa guete'.

Gudaabi' ladxiduá' bi sisi,
gudaa ti bacaanda' do' ndaani' ca bizaluá',
ti bacaanda' do' ziuula' sica ziuula' guendaguti.

Rietenala'dxe' ca bicuininá' be,
ca bicuininá' lase' be,
rabixhinni bizaluá' runi ca beeu guidiruaa be,
nutaabi xhiuubabe naa cué huadxí yanda di'
ne rilué' bila'dxi gue'tu' bigaachi' neegue',
binnibá' ruyadxi guiá', ruyadxi guete',
nisi bieque rudii ra zuguaa xtubi.

Nabani guendarusiaanda',
zándaca runi nga diuxi qui huayati.
Tuungue ná,
pa sou' lu gui
zazou' lu bi, que?

Your Memory

Nostalgia has me boxed
in the stupid wall of this afternoon.
Someone somewhere bastes in happiness
beneath the fresh shade of love.
The earth is like a great comal
over god's hot coals.
Spirits hop across the scalding paths
while a dog tenderly licks
her vulva, then wanders southward.

Console my soul, sea breeze,
spill into my eyes the deepest dream,
a dream dense and distant as death.

I remember your fingers,
your delicate fingers,
my eyes choke on the moons that are your lips,
your memory has nailed me to the lukewarm afternoon
and I'm like the spirit of a body buried yesterday,
a ghost peering in every direction,
vainly searching for the path.

Forgetting exits.
Maybe that's why god never dies.
Who said
if someone can walk over coals
they can also walk over the wind?

Bixidxila' gúdxibe naa
laga cutaabi be guiiba' diidxa'
Sicarú guyé ti'xhi' xquendaranaxhiee',
laga cayabi be naa Ma qui zadu'yanu.

Bixidxi la', binnibá',
pacaa guyé yeyubi dxitaládilu'.

Nanda reza larindxó'
guendarietenala'dxi' xtinne' lu doo
runi bi yooxho' guidiruaabe.

Laugh, please, she told me
while the dagger of the phrase
I wish you all the best sunk into my heart of hearts,
while she told me *we shouldn't see each other anymore.*

Laugh, shadow,
or beat it to look for your skeleton!

My memories' banner
hangs on the clothesline,
tattered by the fierce wind of your tender lips.

Afterword

There is a saying in the diidxazá language of the Zapotec people: 'Hrunadiága' ne hrusiá'nda', hrúuya' ne hriétenaladxe', hrune' ne hriziide' (I hear and I forget, I see and remember, I do and I learn). The luminous poetry of Víctor Terán is a poetry of witnessing and testimonio, a poetry of remembrance and naming, taking the old Zapotec saying to another level. It sings of the beauty and wonders of the world inhabited by the Zapotecs – the 'Cloud People' – in the southern highlands of central Mesoamerica, specifically the Valley of Oaxaca, where they have lived from the late Preclassic Era to the present.

Terán's poetry resonates with a profound emotional depth, encompassing themes of love, birthplace, Zapotec traditions and social justice, to name but a few. His deceptively simple verses and evocative imagery celebrate the beloved's name, body, and soul and the wonders of his birthplace, Juchitán, an almost mythical place that is transformed in his poetry into the 'greatest temple of the Zapotecs, / cordial people who know no fatigue, / tough people unaware of shame.'

In his poetry, there is also space to shed light on the injustices committed by the Mexican Army against activists for rural workers and defenders of indigenous people's rights in the last decades. In 'Soldiers', he writes:

Why,
soldiers,
did you kidnap
a man whose word is as true
as a thorn,
who yearns for
my Juchitán de las flores?

In Terán's poetry, naming is an act of denunciation and rebellion, following a tradition from the Zapotec people as being the first to rebel against the arbitrary actions of colonialism. Terán attempts to name things as urgent tasks in all these poems. He is not only a direct witness of events, places and people from his land but also a wordsmith grappling with his own thoughts and emotions, as we see in the poem 'Your Name':

Day and night, your name.
In the morning, the afternoon, at dusk
only your name spins
through my head
like a man straight-jacketed
for having lost his mind

In Terán's oeuvre, we are repeatedly reminded of the power of naming as an act of defiance and activism. To name a thing is, in the poet's mind, to give it agency and a specific time and place in the world; it is to remember and honour the things treasured by a unique culture and people often marginalised and abused. This profound act of naming in Terán's poetry is a testament to his poetic prowess and his deep understanding of the world around him, but also to his own activism to preserve, promote and enrich a language spoken by almost half a million people that has developed throughout millennia of interaction between the peoples of Mesoamerica.

Through the act of naming, Terán attempts to find a poetic and historical genealogy of a place and its inhabitants, including his direct ancestors, to present-day Mexico, describing his almost fabled city as an all-encompassing universe where all begins. Naming also becomes a form of reverence and devotion. Stories from the past are preserved, a multilayered and multivocal history is expanded, and worldviews where time is viewed as cyclical, not lineal, are shaped through the political act of using Zapotec, as we see in 'Juchitan, My Bride':

Big Juchitan, small Juchitan:
curlew that sings and dances in Zapotec,
loving mother confident to comfort her children,
ancient son of the clouds, my grandfather.

The poet's birthplace's name originally comes from the Nahuatl 'Ixtaxochiltlán', meaning 'Place of the White Flowers', but for many years it was also called Xhavizende, a Zapotecisation of Spanish meaning 'At the feet of San Vicente'. This is a name that, in the poet's work, is to be cherished and proclaimed for everyone to hear: 'How can I not eulogize your name! / How can I not raise the sacred banner of your name on the winds!' Juchitán becomes then a celestial bride of unimaginable proportions, an eternal god and goddess all merged into one, existing high up in the skies, 'father of the hurricane wind, mother of the sun'.

According to Irma Pineda, the Zapotec poet, translator, teacher and defender of indigenous people's rights, the mythical idea of the ancient Zapotecs has been very conducive to developing and cultivating literature and poetry for generations, for they believe themselves to be sons of the roots of ancient trees and wild beasts such as the tiger and the lizard, sons of the rocks and the clouds. Pineda argues[1] that all this fantastic mythology is present in the imagination of the Zapotecs of yesterday and today, helping them to create an extraordinary work of artistic fiction.

In this richly diverse realm of animals, gods and natural elements, we can place the dazzling work of Terán, where the poet, who considers himself a 'native to these lands', carries

1   *La literatura de los binnizá. Zapotecas del istmo*, The National Autonomous University of Mexico (2010)

'Zapotec blood' with a tongue that 'casts wide / the sweetness of its source.'

*

The poet also explores naming the beloved and the various iterations of love, a recurring process often tinged with anxiety, nostalgia and pain. 'I woke with your name stuck in my throat,' he says as he tries to remember an unnerving dream in which the beloved's name appears and disappears as if by magic, like an obscured moon in a night full of humidity that 'suffocates the black sheet of the sky.'

The name of the beloved is everywhere; it follows the poet wherever he goes; it grows like a precious object of desire that accompanies Terán like a persistent memory, refusing to go away: 'I lift a paper, your name. / I put something away, your name.'

But in what ways does naming the loved one and describing her attributes and state of mind constitute a poetic engine for the great poet of Juchitán? What primordial impulses instigate the poet to sing to the beloved with such intensity, clarity and longing?

We can find a link between the specific landscapes, fruits and plants of Oaxaca, the exuberance of its fauna and rivers, and the poet's desire to connect the person he loves with all the wonders of the Zapotec land. In Terán's expanding poetry, the beloved has eyes like 'noble calupin cherries', teeth like 'the white kernels of corn', and between her legs, the soft and creamy fruit of the mamey. She is 'a stag in the air, a raft of flowers / that snakes across the river by morning.' There's high-voltage eroticism and sexual desire in these lines and a wish from the poet to evoke through the loved one's physical and emotional characteristics those of the natural world so interdependent in the Zapotec culture and traditions.

This selection of poems, beautifully rendered into English by Shook, intertwines the Zapotec land, cities, mythology, and the female body to create poetry of outstanding beauty. It unexpectedly links the ethereal with the earthy, the celestial with the terrestrial, taking the reader on a wondrous journey of discovery and the senses that feel timeless.

*

Fittingly and as a proud member of the 'Cloud People', the Zapotec poet also draws attention to the clouds and sky in his poems, naming them in innumerable ways. These clouds, chased by dogs or being generators of life as rain (one of the Zapotec gods), are present throughout this collection, not only as metaphors for passing grief, scattered memories, or harbingers of storms but also as cosmological and philosophical emblems that evoke a direct lineage to Zapotec knowledge and wisdom.

According to Natalia Toledo, a Zapotec poet and activist, numerous Zapotec poets use language that is akin to 'speaking like clouds'. 'Anyone will wonder how one can speak cloud,' she writes. 'The Zapotecs say that the language diidxazá descends from the clouds; diidxa' is word and za cloud, and perhaps because clouds draw different animals and objects in the sky, we Zapotecs know how to draw with words. I can say that part of our identity comes from the clouds. I like this metaphor because clouds adapt to southern Tehuantepec's soft and warm wind but take shape under the brown wind that shakes us in winter. Of course, we are changing beings; clouds pass, and others are formed.'[2]

In Terán's poetry, clouds are allegories for all things changing and evolving, direct links between sky and land, between a

2   *Literatura zapoteca, ¿resistencia o entropía? A modo de respuesta: cuatro escritores binnizá* (1.ª ed.). Universidad Autónoma de la Ciudad de México (2016). This excerpt translated by Leo Boix

unique people and the powers above. Naming them becomes an intrinsic part of an ancient tradition of looking up into the vastness of the sky in an attempt to find answers to some of the biggest questions in life, as he writes in 'From the Palm of My Hand':

The long cloud spanning the horizon –
perhaps you're looking at it,
perhaps you're looking at it now.
My love for you is not the size of that cloud,
not that size.

Leo Boix, London, 2024

Photo: Crispin Hughes

Víctor Terán is the preeminent poet of the Isthmus Zapotec language of southern Oaxaca, Mexico. His work has been translated and anthologized around the world. He has published six books of poetry, including an anthology featuring his translations into Isthmus Zapotec of 40 world poets. In Shook's translation, his work has appeared in *Poetry*, *World Literature Today*, *Modern Poetry in Translation* and *Oxford Magazine*, among others, as well as a Poetry Translation Centre chapbook in 2010. He has been nominated for a Pushcart Prize and featured on BBC4 and KCRW's *Bookworm*. He is co-editor, with Shook, of *Like a New Sun: New Indigenous Poetry from Mexico* (Phoneme Media, 2015), which showcases contemporary poetry written in six of the Indigenous languages of Mexico. Terán's most recent book in English is *The Spines of Love / Ca guichi xti' guendara naxhii* (Gato Negro Ediciones, 2022).

Photo: Travis Elborough   Photo: Naomi Woodis

Shook is a poet, translator and filmmaker, raised in Mexico City and currently living in Northern California. Their debut collection was *Our Obsidian Tongues* (Eyewear Publishing, 2013). Their translations of Indigenous Mexican poetry include work from Nahuatl, which they studied in the village of San Agustín Oapan, Guerrero, and Mikeas Sánchez's *How to Be a Good Savage and Other Poems* (Milkweed Editions, 2024), co-translated from Zoque and Spanish with Wendy Call.

Leo Boix is a bilingual Latinx poet born in Argentina who lives in the UK. His debut English collection, *Ballad of a Happy Immigrant* (Chatto & Windus, 2021), was a Poetry Book Society Wild Card Choice. His second English collection, *Southernmost: Sonnets*, is forthcoming with Chatto & Windus in 2025. Boix has also published two poetry collections in Spanish, *Un Lugar Propio* (2015) and *Mar de Noche* (2017), both with Letras del Sur Editora, Argentina. He has translated many Latin American poets into English, including Diana Bellessi, José Watanabe, Cecilia Vicuña, Oscar David López and Jorge Eduardo Eielson.

About the Poetry Translation Centre

Set up in 2004, the Poetry Translation Centre is the only UK organisation dedicated to translating, publishing and promoting contemporary poetry from Africa, Asia, the Middle East and Latin America. We introduce extraordinary poets from around the world to new audiences through books, online resources and bilingual events. We champion diversity and representation in the arts and forge enduring relations with diaspora communities in the UK. We explore the craft of translation through our long-running programme of workshops which are open to all.

The Poetry Translation Centre is based in London and is an Arts Council National Portfolio organisation. To find out more about us, including how you can support our work, please visit: www.poetrytranslation.org.

About the World Poet Series

The *World Poet Series* offers an introduction to some of the world's most exciting contemporary poets in an elegant pocket-sized format. The books are presented as dual-language editions, with the English and original-language text displayed side by side. They include specially commissioned translations and completing each book is an afterword essay by an English-language poet, responding to the translations.